FLYING START SCIENCE

HEAT

Kim Taylor

Belitha Press

Contents

Designed by **Teresa Foster** and **Tony Potter**, **Times Four Publishing Ltd**

Illustrated by **Peter Bull**

Science adviser: **Richard Oels** Warden Park School, Cuckfield, Sussex.

First published in Great Britain in 1993 by
Belitha Press Ltd
31 Newington Green,
London, N16 9PU

Reprinted in 1994.

Text © Kim Taylor Times Four Publishing Ltd 1993.
Photographs © Kim Taylor and Jane Burton 1993
(except where credited elsewhere).
Design and illustration © Belitha Press and Times Four
Publishing Ltd 1993.
Format © Belitha Press Ltd 1993.

British Library Cataloguing in Publication Data: CIP data for this
book is available from the British Library.

ISBN 1 85561 165 1 (Hardback)
ISBN 1 85561 166 X (Paperback)

Printed in China for Imago

Origination by Bright Arts, Hong Kong
Typeset by Amber Graphics, Burgess Hill

About this book

Why is the sun hot? What is really happening to wood when it burns? How do birds measure the heat of their eggs? Why does ice cream melt on a hot fruit pie? And what *is* heat, anyway?

In this book you can find out the answers to these, and many other, fascinating questions. You can read about heat from the sun, and learn about the Earth's own heat that spills out in volcanoes and boiling pools. Find out how animals keep themselves warm, and how they cope in hot places. Discover, too, how important heat is in the modern world and how people have discovered many ways to create it for themselves.

Warning!

All experiments with heat can be dangerous. NEVER EXPERIMENT WITH MATCHES, FIRE OR OTHER HOT THINGS UNLESS AN ADULT IS HELPING YOU.

What is heat?

Everything is made of tiny particles too small to see, even with the most powerful microscope. When something is hot, its particles vibrate (move about). The hotter it is, the more the particles vibrate.

Heat is a kind of **energy**. It always passes from hot things to cold things and never the other way. For example, if you put ice cream on a hot fruit pie, heat from the pie passes into the ice cream and melts it. The pie gets cooler and the ice cream gets warmer.

The heat of the sun

Our sun is a star – a very hot ball of gas. Most of the heat on Earth comes from the energy that radiates from the sun. Without its heat, nothing on Earth could live.

Hot spots

The hottest parts of the Earth's surface are the areas of land where the sun's rays are most strong. During the day, these rocks in the Namib Desert in Africa are hot enough to cook an egg on. Most desert animals spend the hottest part of the day in the shade.

Heat is produced when something is burned. In this bonfire the burning wood combines with oxygen gas in the air to make heat. Flames are made by the burning gases that are given off by the wood as it is heated.

Hot hot hot!

Everything on Earth contains some heat. Even the particles in an iceberg are vibrating a little with heat energy. Although there is a minimum temperature (absolute zero, or minus 273° C) there is no known maximum temperature. The temperature at the centre of the sun is about 15 million° C! But people can survive only when their body temperature is between about 30° and 40° C. Outside these limits it is either too cold or too hot and they soon die.

Burning gas produces heat. These extremely hot **oxyacetylene** flames are being used to cut through a great slab of steel. They reach 3300° C.

Electricity can produce heat. This electric spark is so hot it is being used to **weld** pieces of steel together. The spark reaches temperatures above 3500° C.

Did you know?

Death Valley, California, is one of the world's hottest places. Temperatures over 48° C (120° F) have been recorded there.

Making heat

Heat can be made in many different ways, each one using some kind of energy. An electric fire uses **electrical energy**, changing it into heat. A wood or coal fire uses **chemical energy**. We make body heat ourselves, using chemical energy stored in the food we eat. Huge amounts of **nuclear energy** are stored in some substances, such as uranium. This can be changed into heat in nuclear power stations.

The heat from a candle flame melts the wax of the candle, turning some of the wax into **vapour** (a gas). This gas, burning with the oxygen in the air, produces heat and light. On page 11 you can find out what happens to a flame when no more oxygen is left.

Heat experiment

FACT OR FRICTION?

You need
● A pen or pencil

1 Hold the pen or pencil firmly in one hand and rub it back and forth quickly on your sleeve, skirt or trouser leg.

2 After about 5 seconds of rubbing, hold the pen to your lips. Can you feel the part that has been rubbed?

Friction is the force that tries to stop things sliding over each other. Energy is needed to overcome this force, and the energy is turned into heat.

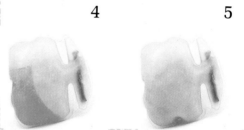

Crystallizing heat

When a liquid forms **crystals**, it gives off heat. Here you can see the inside of a handwarmer (1) – a device to help people keep warm in cold places. It contains a special liquid. When the red plastic rod is bent (2) crystals start to form and spread right through until the liquid is all crystallized (5). This makes the bag warm to hold.

1

2

3

4   5

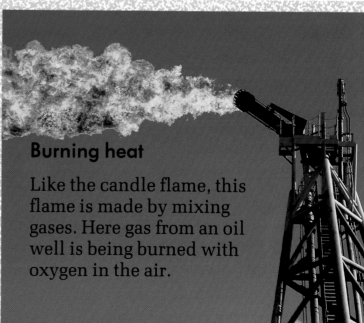

Burning heat

Like the candle flame, this flame is made by mixing gases. Here gas from an oil well is being burned with oxygen in the air.

Friction heat

Heat can be produced by rubbing things together. This is because of a force called **friction**. This fast car's tyres, spinning against the road surface, are hot because of friction.

Human heat

Hard physical work makes you feel hot. This is because your muscles turn energy from your food into heat energy as well as movement. This sportsman is hot because he has been running fast. People's bodies sweat to cool down (see page 20).

Electricity is a form of energy. When it is made to pass through a thin wire, as in this electric fire, some of it is turned into heat. The wire glows with heat and helps to warm up a room.

Did you know?

Birds burn up food fast to provide energy for flying, so their body temperatures are usually higher than mammals'. Sparrows, for example, are 4° C warmer than people!

Measuring heat

Heat can be measured in two different ways – as temperature (hotness) or as the amount of heat energy something contains (see page 9). Thermometers are instruments that are used to measure temperature. Some are marked with measurements in degrees Celsius (° C). Water freezes at 0° C and boils at 100° C. Some thermometers are marked in degrees Fahrenheit (° F). Water freezes at 32° F and boils at 212° F.

This baby chicken is just hatching out. An egg has to be kept at an exact temperature in order to hatch. A mother hen can judge the temperature of her eggs to within half a degree, using a bare patch of skin on her chest, called the brood patch.

Did you know?

The ancient Egyptians hatched chicken's eggs in mud huts heated by fires. They judged the heat of the eggs by holding them against their cheeks.

Heat experiment

HOT LIPS

You need
- Two mugs
- Two teaspoons
- Thermometer
- Warm and cold water

1 Fill both mugs with a mixture of warm and cold water. Put slightly more warm water in one mug than the other.

2 Take the temperature of each mug of water, adding small amounts of warm or cold water until one is about 5° C warmer than the other.

3 Put a teaspoon in each mug and leave them there for at least half a minute. Take the spoons out in turn and hold each for a second against the tip of your finger. Can you tell which is the warmer spoon?

4 Put the spoons back in the water for half a minute. Then test them against the back of your hand. Repeat, testing the spoons against your lips. Which can judge differences in temperature best, fingers, hands or lips?

These thermometers measure temperature in various ways.

This medical thermometer contains a thin tube filled with mercury – a liquid metal. Mercury expands and rises up the tube when it heats up.

This thermometer contains alcohol (coloured blue). When it is heated, the alcohol expands and rises inside the glass tube.

This is an aquarium thermometer. It contains special dyes that change colour as they are heated. The green window shows the temperature of the water in the aquarium.

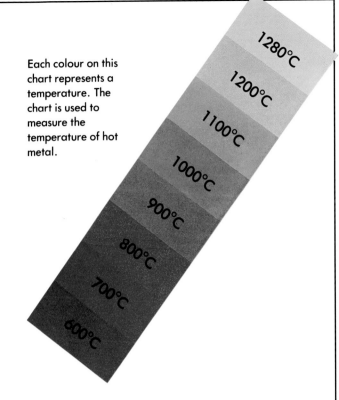

Each colour on this chart represents a temperature. The chart is used to measure the temperature of hot metal.

1280°C
1200°C
1100°C
1000°C
900°C
800°C
700°C
600°C

Colour temperature

The steel bar on the left is at about 1100° C. The colour chart (above) can be used to judge the temperature of hot metal. That is because metal changes colour as it is heated. It starts to glow red when it reaches 600° C. As it gets hotter its colour changes to orange and then to yellow. Finally it becomes white hot.

Heat energy

Temperature and heat energy are not the same thing. If you add a teaspoon of very hot water to a bowl of cold water, it will not make much difference to the temperature of the water in the bowl. However, if you add a glassful of warm water, this *will* make a difference because the water in the glass contains more heat. The water in the glass is at a lower *temperature* than the water in the spoon, but it contains more *heat energy*.

Fire

When something burns, it combines with oxygen in the air. Heat and gas are produced. You can see and feel the heat. The gas is clear, so you cannot see it. Smoke is often formed, too. It is made of tiny particles that have not completely burned.

1 Dry leaves and twigs contain a lot of **carbon**. Fire spreads through them quickly.

2 Heat from burning twigs turns part of the other twigs into gas, which burns as a sheet of flame.

3 When the gas is all burned the bigger branches have been turned to **charcoal**, which is almost pure carbon. It glows red hot.

4 All that is left is soft powdery **ash**. It consists of chemicals in the wood that will not burn.

Firefighting

Petrol is very dangerous because it lights easily. But even petrol fires can only burn if they are supplied with oxygen. Thick foam from a fire hose stops oxygen getting to the surface of the petrol and so the fire is put out.

Did you know?

It is thought that people first learned to make fire for themselves about 450,000 years ago.

Heat experiment

FLINT AND STEEL

You could also try this with a lighter flint and a nail file.

You need
- A lump of flint from a road or beach
- A file

1 In a dimly lit or dark room try striking the flint against the file. Make the flint slide a bit over the rough surface of the file. With practice you should be able to produce sparks.

In the first picture (above left) you can see a lighted candle floating on water, with a glass jar over it. As the flame burns, it uses up the oxygen in the jar. On the right you can see the same candle a short time afterwards. Water has been sucked in to replace the oxygen, making the water level rise. All the oxygen in the jar has been used up, so the flame has gone out.

Friction of flint on steel produces so much heat in one spot that bits of file are heated red hot and fly off as sparks. People used flints to light fires before matches were invented.

Solar heat

Heat travels from the sun through space as **electro-magnetic waves.** By the time these waves reach Earth they have spread out and are not burning hot. Nearer the sun, the planet Venus is extremely hot all the time. Further from the sun, Mars is too cold for life.

Plant leaves, like this oak leaf, collect heat and light from the sun. They use light energy to make plant food from carbon dioxide gas in the air. Heat from the sun warms the leaves to speed their growth.

Energy from the sun

The sun is a star – a glowing ball of very hot gas. Its heat comes from deep inside, where atoms of hydrogen gas crash together. As they do so, energy is released.

The sun's heat warms the Earth and produces the weather, making currents of air move and so causing winds and rainfall. You can find out more about this on pages 24-25.

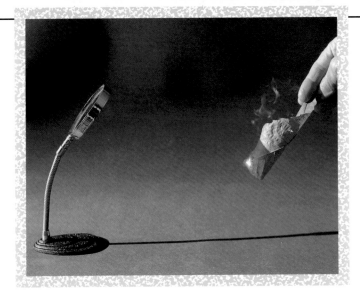

When the sun's rays pass through a lens they can be focused onto a small spot that becomes very bright and very hot. Here a lens is focusing light onto a dead leaf, which is beginning to smoke as the sun's rays heat it up.

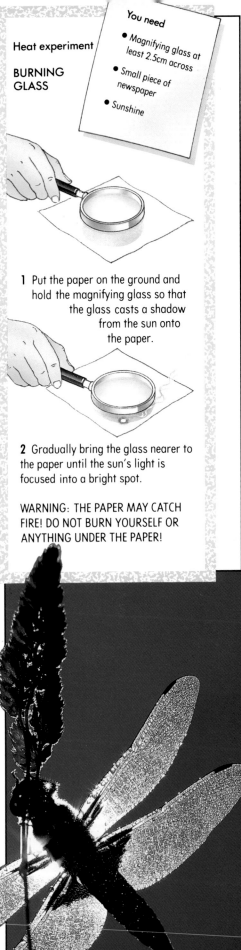

Heat experiment

BURNING GLASS

You need
• Magnifying glass at least 2.5cm across
• Small piece of newspaper
• Sunshine

1 Put the paper on the ground and hold the magnifying glass so that the glass casts a shadow from the sun onto the paper.

2 Gradually bring the glass nearer to the paper until the sun's light is focused into a bright spot.

WARNING: THE PAPER MAY CATCH FIRE! DO NOT BURN YOURSELF OR ANYTHING UNDER THE PAPER!

Dark objects absorb more heat than light-coloured ones. These rocks in a desert in Africa are almost black. They absorb heat from the sun during the day and become too hot to touch. Even so, some orange lichens can grow on them.

Solar flare

The sun's surface temperature is about 5500° C. The temperature inside is far greater (see page 5). Here you can see a huge solar flare – an explosion on the surface throwing particles far out into space.

The sun's heat is very important to cold-blooded animals because it provides them with warmth (see pages 18-19). This dragonfly is drying its damp wings and warming its body so that it can fly.

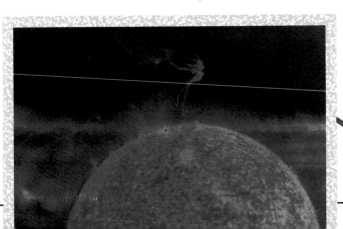

13

Earth heat

The centre of the Earth, its core, is very hot. Some of the core is liquid white hot iron at 2000° C. Nearer the surface there is red hot liquid rock called magma. Magma sometimes flows up to the surface where there are cracks in the Earth's crust. It flows out as lava.

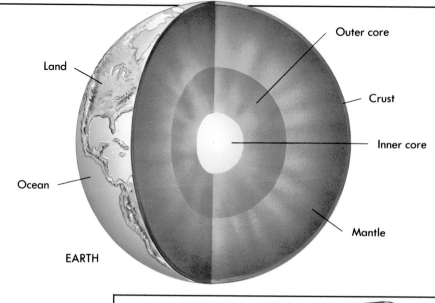

Land

Ocean

EARTH

Outer core

Crust

Inner core

Mantle

Did you know?

Deep mines become so hot due to Earth heat that miners would roast if there were no air-conditioning.

Volcanoes

Volcanoes are formed when there is a crack in the Earth's surface. Red hot magma shoots out from the inside of the Earth when a volcano erupts, as this one is doing in Hawaii. It forms a glowing hot river of lava. Even during the day (below) you can see the lava flowing down the mountain.

Heat from inside the Earth can also seep to the surface and cause mud pools to boil. This happens where the Earth's crust is thin. As the mud bubbles burst they form strange shapes. There are famous boiling mud pools in Iceland and New Zealand.

Earth power

Where the Earth's crust is thin it is possible to build power stations to use the heat energy below the ground.

This power station in New Zealand uses the Earth's natural heat to produce power to heat and light homes.

In places where the Earth's inner heat is near the surface, rocks and water heat up. Sometimes steam comes spurting out of the ground in a **geyser**. Some geysers spurt all the time, while others spurt only from time to time. This geyser is squirting up through a pool of water, so the steam carries water up into the air with it.

Heat experiment

SODA GEYSER

You need
- Small wide-mouthed bottle or jar with a plastic lid
- Drinking straw
- Sticky tape
- Vinegar
- Bicarbonate of soda

1 Ask an adult to make a hole in the lid of the bottle so the straw fits tightly.

2 Push the straw in so its end is about 2cm above the bottom of the bottle. Fix it firmly to the lid with sticky tape.

3 Three-quarters fill the bottle with cold water and add 1-2 tablespoons of vinegar.

NOW PUT THE BOTTLE IN THE KITCHEN SINK OR DO THE REST OF THE EXPERIMENT OUTDOORS!

4 Put a teaspoon of bicarbonate of soda into the bottle, while a friend quickly puts on the lid.

Acid in the vinegar acts on the bicarbonate of soda to make carbon dioxide gas. This causes water and bubbles to squirt out like a geyser.

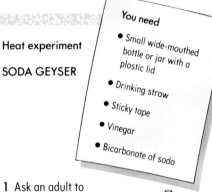

Plant warmth

In order to grow, plants need warmth, which they get from the sun. Very few plants can make their own warmth. However, plant material can be turned into warmth by **bacteria** and **fungi**. They can rot a pile of dead leaves, making it warm up and even start to steam. In fact, if hay is stacked up when it is too green and fresh it can heat up so much that it catches fire!

Snake hatch

Female grass snakes often lay their eggs in a heap of dead leaves. As the leaves rot they heat up, gently warming the eggs. The young snakes cut slits in the soft egg shells and look out as they hatch.

Did you know?

An Australian bird, the Mallee Fowl, builds a pile of leaves which rot, making enough heat to hatch its eggs. The bird adjusts the temperature by adding or removing leaves.

Plants in hot places

Cactus plants are mostly found in hot climates. This candelabra cactus is well equipped to withstand the extreme heat and dryness of the Mexican desert. Its swollen stems contain a supply of water. The stems absorb heat and become warm during the day.

Heat experiment

COMPOST

You need

- Large tough polythene bag
- Expanded polystyrene box, or other insulated container
- Freshly cut grass
- Thermometer

1 Collect fresh grass cuttings from a park, garden or playing field. Pack the cuttings into the polythene bag.

2 Put the bag into the insulated container and leave it overnight.

3 Next morning, measure the temperature of the air outside the box. Then put the thermometer right into the middle of the bag of grass. Compare the two temperatures.

4 Record the temperature of the compost each morning for a few days. Does it rise or fall?

M	T	W	Th	F	S	Su
72	74	76				

Bacteria and fungi start to work as soon as grass is cut. They break down the grass, making carbon dioxide gas and heat.

The temperature inside a heap of rotting plant material rises as bacteria and fungi get to work. The middle of the heap can become too hot for animals to live in. Worms live in the part that is just the right heat for them.

The arum (below) is one of the few plants that make heat. When the flower first opens the spadix (the tall pointed brown piece in the middle) is warm to touch. The warmth helps to attract small insects that fall into the flower and are trapped. They are later released, covered in pollen.

When dead leaves sink to the bottom of a pond they rot and give off heat and gas. The gas bubbles up to the surface. It may be **methane**, which will burn with a blue flame if you light it.

Warming up

People and animals make heat in their bodies. The heat comes from the food they eat when it combines with oxygen in the body **cells**. This process is like burning (see pages 10-11) but is slower. The food is burned to make heat and muscle power. Warm-blooded animals make heat all the time, even when they are still. Cold-blooded animals can make heat only when they move. The more active an animal is, the more heat it makes.

This tiger moth is at rest on a flower.

Now it buzzes its wings, ready for take-off.

Moth sloth

Some moths, and some other insects, cannot fly at all until their bodies have warmed up. The tiger moth (top) is unable to take off even when danger threatens. It first has to buzz its wings for half a minute or so (above). Buzzing works the wing muscles, making enough heat to warm the body. Then the moth can fly.

Shivering snakes!

Snakes are cold-blooded animals so they can make their own heat only when they move about. But a mother python has to keep her eggs warm so that they will hatch. She does this by curling her body around the eggs and shivering to make heat. This baby python has just hatched. It is very fierce.

18

Hot dogs

Warm-blooded animals, like these dogs, make a lot of heat when they run. Blood carries oxygen and food energy to the muscles. The muscles work the legs back and forth, so they move and produce heat.

Some cold-blooded animals, like this chameleon, warm up their bodies by basking in the sun until they are really hot. A nicely warmed-up lizard or chameleon can act quickly when in danger, but a cold one is sluggish and may get caught.

Did you know?

Rattlesnakes have heat sensors on their heads so sensitive that they can detect the body of an animal nearby even if it is less than $1°\,C$ warmer than its surroundings.

Cooling down

Too much heat can be a problem. Small animals can hide underground during the day. Larger animals find a cool place to sit or stand. Animals can also make their bodies lose heat. Elephants, rabbits and the fennec fox (see the opposite page) lose heat through their large ears. Humans lose heat by sweating.

A black dog gets hotter in the sun than a brown dog because black absorbs more heat. So the black dog has to lie in the shade to keep cool.

Running shower

When your body is hot, water or sweat **evaporating** from the skin takes heat from your body and cools you down. A shower from a bottle is very cooling, as this runner knows.

Did you know?

Many mammals, birds and some reptiles cool down by panting. This allows water to evaporate from the mouth and lungs.

Hippos keep cool by spending the day in the water. The river water flowing past their bodies cools them down. At night they come out to feed.

This fennec (a desert fox) is well adapted to life in the African desert. Its enormous ears give it a large area from which it can lose heat, and so keep cool.

In hot places where there is little shade, people tend to wear *more* clothes, not fewer, to keep themselves cool. This man belongs to the Tuareg people of the Sahara Desert. The long flowing robes protect him from the sun's heat.

Keeping cool

These houses are cool inside because they have small windows, which do not let in much sunshine, and the walls are painted white. White reflects the sun's heat back into the sky.

Heat experiment

ON REFLECTION...

You need
- Black card
- White card
- Scissors
- Electric lamp

1 Cut out a rectangular piece of black card about 2cm × 3cm. Cut out another from white card, the same size.

2 Make a fold 1cm from the end of each piece of card. Open out the folds at right angles.

3 Pick both cards up by the right-angled pieces and hold them so they are about 5cm away from the heat of an electric lamp. Keep them there for at least 5 seconds. Now feel them with your lips. Which card is warmer? Why do you think this is?

Moving heat

Heat energy always moves from hot things to cold things, but it can do so in various ways. It can travel through some materials such as metal quite easily. This is called **conduction**. Heat can move by **radiation** – travelling in rays through air and space at the speed of light. Heat can also move in currents of warm air or water. This is called **convection**. A hot drink in a cup loses heat by all three methods – by conduction into a spoon, or the table on which it sits, by radiation into the room where it is absorbed by the walls, and by convection into the air.

Conduction experiment

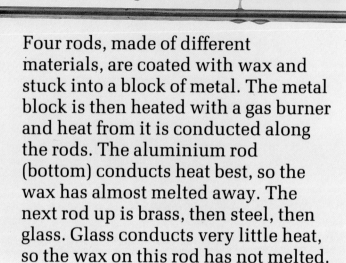

Four rods, made of different materials, are coated with wax and stuck into a block of metal. The metal block is then heated with a gas burner and heat from it is conducted along the rods. The aluminium rod (bottom) conducts heat best, so the wax has almost melted away. The next rod up is brass, then steel, then glass. Glass conducts very little heat, so the wax on this rod has not melted.

Did you know?

Silver conducts heat so well that a solid silver teaspoon in a hot drink becomes too hot to hold.

Animal warmth

Heat from the body of this bird sitting on her nest passes into her eggs to keep them warm. This is essential if her eggs are to hatch out successfully.

Heat experiment

PIN DROP

You need
- Copper wire
- Steel wire
- Pliers
- A mug
- 8 pins
- Petroleum jelly
- Hot water
- Newspaper

1 Cut one 150 mm length of copper wire and another, the same length, of steel wire.

2 Use pliers to bend each wire at right angles, 60 mm from one end. Bend the shorter arms back on themselves about 20 mm from the right angle.

3 Hang the bent wires on the edge of the mug. Stand the mug on newspaper.

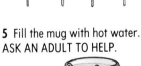

4 Smear the tops of the pins with petroleum jelly and stick them along the wires.

5 Fill the mug with hot water. ASK AN ADULT TO HELP.

6 Watch what happens. Heat is conducted along the wires and melts the petroleum jelly, causing the pins to fall. Which pins drop off first. Which wire conducts heat quicker?

Hot black

Heat from the sun is absorbed by black rocks, so they get very hot. If you put your hand on one of these rocks during the day you would find it felt hotter than the light-coloured rocks around it. The paler rocks reflect the heat and so stay cooler.

Still air conducts very little heat away. Soft fur, like that on this rat, traps still air and keeps the animal warm. However, water conducts heat away, and uses heat when it evaporates, so an animal with wet fur will soon feel cold. It is important for this small animal to dry its fur quickly, or it will get chilled.

Waste heat

An open fire is very wasteful of heat energy. Three-quarters of the heat goes up the chimney by convection. Only one quarter warms the room by radiation.

23

Hot air

As air is heated it expands and rises. Air over land heats up more quickly than air over the sea. As the warm overland air rises, cool air rushes in off the sea to take its place.

That is why on sunny days there is nearly always a sea breeze by the coast. In this picture, clouds have formed from the warm air rising just above a small island.

Air burn

Really hot air looks the same as cold air, so you have to be careful when using a blower to strip paint. Coils of wire made red hot by electricity heat up the air inside the blower so that it comes out hot enough to melt paint.

Shimmering heat

Hot air is less dense than cold air. When the two meet and mix you can often see a shimmering effect. This is because light is bent when it passes from one density to another.

Did you know?

Hot-air balloons can rise up to 10,000 metres above the ground.

Clouds, wind and rain

The sun's heat drives the Earth's weather, making winds blow, clouds gather and rain fall. Clouds form when warm, damp air rises into cooler air. The water vapour in the warm air **condenses** into tiny droplets, forming a cloud. If the cloud goes on rising, more water condenses and the droplets get bigger. Then they start to fall as rain.

Heat experiment

UP UP AND AWAY

You need
- Tissue paper
- Scissors
- An old plate
- Matches

ASK AN ADULT TO HELP YOU.
DO NOT USE MATCHES ON YOUR OWN.

1 Cut out a piece of tissue paper about 10cm × 20cm. Curl it round to make a tube.

2 Stand the tube on a plate. Light the top of the tube with a match. Watch what happens!

As the flame burns down the paper, it makes a rising column of hot air above it. When the paper is all turned to ash it is so light it gets sucked up into the rising warm air.

The flame from a gas blowlamp is mostly very hot air. Gas burns with a blue flame when it has plenty of oxygen. If it is starved of oxygen the flame turns yellow and sooty.

Storing heat

It is not easy to store heat, because it is always trying to escape. It eventually escapes even through thick layers of **insulation**. But other forms of energy can be stored and later turned into heat. Food is a source of energy, so a food store can be a heat store. Animals store food in their bodies as fat. Fat is not only a good insulator but it can also be turned into body heat.

Heat experiment

SOME KEEP IT HOT!

You need
- Two small jars with lids
- One large jar with a lid
- Newspaper
- A wide-mouthed vacuum flask
- Ice cubes

1 Tear up enough pieces of newspaper to make an insulating layer in the big jar.

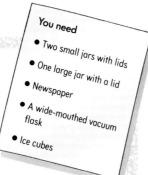

2 Put equal numbers of ice cubes in the two small jars and the vacuum flask. Screw the lids on tightly.

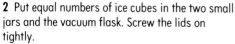

3 Put one small jar inside the large jar and quickly pack the newspaper all around it. Screw the lid on the big jar.

4 Wait until the ice in the jar you can see is melted. Unpack the other jar. Are the ice cubes in it still frozen? How much ice is there in the vacuum flask?

The newspaper is a good insulator. It keeps heat from the ice.

Hot flask

A vacuum flask slows down the escape of heat. The inner container is made of two layers of silvered glass separated by a **vacuum**. As there is no air in a vacuum, heat does not escape across the gap. A little heat is lost by radiation from the silvery glass, and more escapes through the top, but a drink can stay hot inside for hours.

This machine is digging coal out of the ground. **Fossil fuels** (coal, oil and gas) are all the remains of plants and animals that lived millions of years ago. They collected energy from the sun and that energy is still there. When we use these fuels, we release the stored energy as heat.

Body warmth

Warm-blooded sea animals need to be well insulated so that their body heat does not escape into the cold water. They have a layer of fat, called **blubber**, under the skin to keep the heat inside. This baby seal is warm inside a furry coat with its lining of blubber.

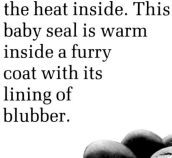

Heat trap

The silvery plastic sheeting around this tired marathon runner reflects heat from his body back towards him. It stops him getting chilled after the race.

This hornet is having a quick meal of sugar water. The sugar will be converted into energy so that the hornet can buzz its wings and fly. It has to feed often because it can store very little energy.

Food stores

Some small animals, like this mouse, store food for winter. The mouse is able to keep warm in the cold weather by eating its food store.

The effects of heat

Heat makes some things expand, which means they get bigger. A metal rod is slightly longer when it is hot than when it is cold. The amount of expansion depends on the kind of metal. Heat also makes solids melt and liquids boil.

Mud crackers

Heat dries things out by evaporating the water they contain. The sun's heat dried up this mud. The mud shrank as it dried, leaving a pattern of cracks. If you imagine water poured into the cracks, you can get an idea of how much water it once contained.

Spread your wings

Birds that dive for fish, as this cormorant does, cannot fly when their wing feathers are soaked. They spread out their wings and dry themselves in the sun so they can fly again.

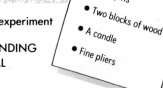

You need
- Two paper clips
- Two pins
- Two blocks of wood
- A candle
- Fine pliers

Heat experiment

EXPANDING METAL

1 Use the pliers to straighten the paper clips. One will be your expander and the other will be your pointer. Bend one end of each into a small loop to fit the pins. Give the pointer a longer loop, as shown.

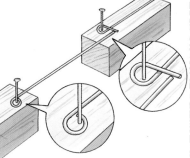

2 Pin the pointer on one block of wood and the expander on the other so the end of the expander rests against the loop of the pointer.

3 Carefully move the blocks together until the pointer starts to move.

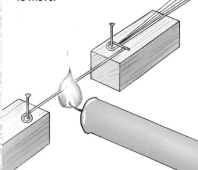

4 Light the candle and use it to heat the expander. Watch the tip of the pointer.

Heat causes the expander to expand and push against the loop of the pointer. The pointer is a sensitive lever, so a tiny movement at the loop end makes the tip of the pointer move much more.

Because metal expands when it heats up, railway lines used to have gaps in them at regular intervals. This allowed the rails to expand in hot weather without buckling the rail and causing an accident. Modern rails are treated in a special way so there is very little expansion. This gives rail passengers a smoother and quieter ride.

Did you know?

The eggs of some reptiles (particularly turtles and alligators) can develop into either males or females depending on the temperature at which they are kept.

Heat speeds up chemical processes. This tortoise egg has been laid in the ground. The number of days it will take to hatch depends on the temperature. The warmer it is the sooner the chemical processes inside the egg can take place and hatching can follow.

Heat makes liquids boil. When they boil, they turn into gas. Here, heat from a flame is boiling a flask of water. You can see clear bubbles of steam (which is water gas) rising from the bottom.

When water boils in a kettle, steam comes out of the spout. At first the steam is clear, but as it quickly cools to below boiling point (100° C) it condenses into a cloud of tiny droplets, as here.

The uses of heat

Humans first discovered how to make fire thousands of years ago. It was one of the greatest discoveries, because it enabled people to keep warm, to cook food so it could be more easily digested and preserved, to make pottery utensils and to form metals into tools and weapons.

Today heat is used in these and many other ways. The most important use is to provide the modern world with energy. When fuels are burned, heat is released. This heat can be turned into other kinds of energy, such as electricity, to light and heat homes and offices. Or it can be used in engines to drive cars, aircraft, trains and other forms of transport.

A horse being shod was a common sight in the days before cars. This man is fitting a hot iron shoe onto the hoof of a horse. The shoe is so hot that it makes the hoof smoke. Earlier, he had heated the shoe until it was red hot. Then he hammered it to fit the hoof.

Bonfires

Fire was very important to early peoples. Often it must have meant the difference between life and death for them in cold weather. Some old festivals survive at which fires are lit and people look forward again to the days of summer when the sun will heat the land.

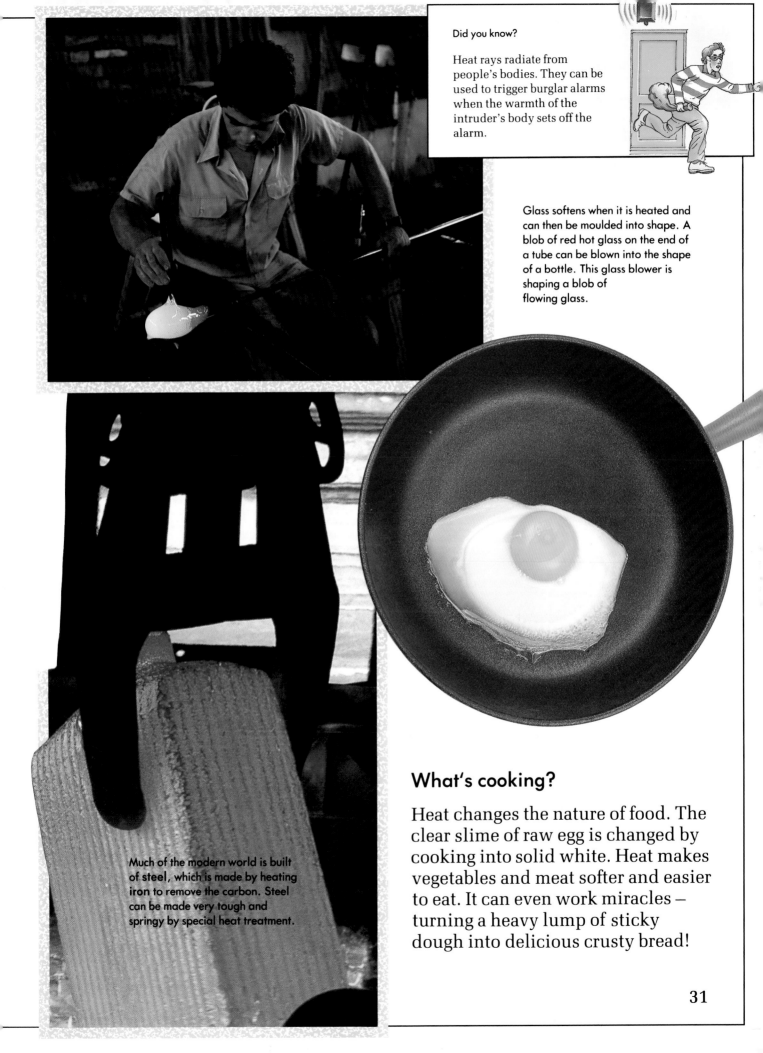

Glass softens when it is heated and can then be moulded into shape. A blob of red hot glass on the end of a tube can be blown into the shape of a bottle. This glass blower is shaping a blob of flowing glass.

Much of the modern world is built of steel, which is made by heating iron to remove the carbon. Steel can be made very tough and springy by special heat treatment.

What's cooking?

Heat changes the nature of food. The clear slime of raw egg is changed by cooking into solid white. Heat makes vegetables and meat softer and easier to eat. It can even work miracles — turning a heavy lump of sticky dough into delicious crusty bread!

Heat words

Ash Powdery unburned chemicals left behind after something has been burned.

Bacteria Microscopic creatures.

Blubber Fat layer under the skin of some animals.

Carbon Substance found in all animals and plants. Coal is mainly carbon.

Cells All living things are made up of tiny units called cells. A human body contains millions.

Charcoal A form of carbon made by heating wood.

Chemical energy Energy contained in chemicals.

Condense To turn from a gas into a liquid.

Conduction Movement of heat through something. Heat is conducted from a hot drink through a teaspoon into your fingers.

Convection Movement of heat as a result of rising currents of air or water.

Crystals Solids with regular geometric shapes.

Electrical energy Energy in the form of electricity.

Electro-magnetic waves Waves that travel through the air or through space. Heat, light and radio are electro-magnetic waves.

Energy Power or force needed to move something.

Evaporate To change from liquid or solid to a gas.

Fossil fuels Gas, oil and coal.

Friction A force that tries to stop things sliding over each other.

Fungi Plants with no leaves, flowers or green colouring. Mushrooms are fungi.

Geyser A natural hot spring that shoots water and steam into the air.

Insulation Material that slows the loss of heat.

Iron A metal, mined from the ground and used to make cast iron, steel etc.

Methane A colourless, odourless inflammable gas that contains carbon.

Nuclear energy Energy obtained by splitting (or joining together) the tiny particles of which substances are made.

Oxyacetylene A mixture of the gases oxygen and acetylene, which burns with a very hot flame.

Radiate/Radiation To travel outwards in waves.

Vacuum An empty space, with the air removed.

Vapour A gas formed from something that is normally a liquid or a solid.

Weld To heat metals so they melt together.

Index

PICTURE CREDITS

All photographs are by Kim Taylor and Jane Burton except for those supplied by Eye Ubiquitous: *title page, 6 bottom, 7 top, inset* and *bottom, 15 top left* and *bottom, 20 bottom left, 23 bottom right, 27 centre right, 30 top;* Tony Potter: *20-21 centre, 30 bottom;* Zefa: *cover, 3, 5 centre, 9 top left, 11 top, 12 bottom, 13 bottom, 14 bottom left* and *right, 21 top right, 24 bottom left, 26 bottom, 31 top* and *bottom.*